THE
THOROUGHBRED
HORSE

B O R N · T O · R U N

by Gail B. Stewart

Illustrated with photographs
by Ron Colbroth

Reading consultant:

John Manning, Professor of Reading
University of Minnesota

Capstone Press
M I N N E A P O L I S

Printed in the United States of America.

Capstone Press • 2440 Fernbrook Lane • Minneapolis, MN 55447

Editorial Director   John Coughlan
Managing Editor   John Martin
Copy Editor   Gil Chandler

Library of Congress Cataloging-in-Publication Data

Stewart, Gail, 1949-
  The thoroughbred horse : born to run / by Gail B. Stewart.
    p. cm.--
  Includes bibliographical references and index.
  ISBN 1-56065-245-4
  1. Thoroughbred horse--Juvenile literature. [1. Thoroughbred horse. 2. Race horses.]   I. Title.
SF293.T5S765   1995
636.1'32--dc20   94-22830
                                              CIP
                                               AC

ISBN: 1-56065-245-4

99 98 97 96 95   8 7 6 5 4 3 2 1

Table of Contents

Quick Facts about the Thoroughbred Horse

Description

Height:	15 to 17 **hands** (equal to four-inch [ten-centimeter] segments) from the ground to the top of the shoulders. That works out to between 60 and 68 inches (150 and 170 centimeters) tall.
Weight:	900 to 1,200 lbs. (408 to 544 kilograms).
Physical features:	tall with long, straight legs. They have long, slender necks and large eyes. The horse has a full chest, with a large heart and lungs.
Colors:	solid colors (never **pinto** or spotted) including black, gray, **chestnut**, **roan**, or brown.

Development

History of breed:	descended from crosses between large English horses and three Arabian or Turk stallions.
Place of origin:	England
Numbers:	the American Jockey Club registers 50,000 new Thoroughbreds each year.

Food

Thoroughbreds have a very controlled diet and eat three times a day. The largest meal is at noon. A Thoroughbred eats corn, **bran**, oats, carrots, molasses, and a regular dose of vitamins. Thoroughbreds need at least 12 gallons (45.5 liters) of water each day.

Life History

Life span: a well-cared-for Thoroughbred may live from 20 to 30 years.

Reproductive life: **stallions** (male horses) are bred when they are about two years old; **mares** (female horses) when they are three or four. Thoroughbred mares carry their **foals** for 11 months before giving birth.

Uses

Thoroughbreds are used for track racing, for **polo**, for **dressage** and other horse show-competitions, for jumping, and for pleasure riding.

Chapter 1

The Fastest Creature on Earth

It is a sunny, dry day at the racetrack. A bell sounds. The pounding of hooves can be heard at a distance. A cloud of dust and dirt flies from the track. A galloping herd of brown and black horses suddenly comes around the turn. Urged on by his rider, the lead horse is heading straight for the finish line–and a fortune for his owner.

These horses are tall, and their legs seem too long for their bodies. But they can run like the wind. They are called Thoroughbreds.

The name can be confusing. Some people say "thoroughbred" when they really mean "**purebred**," a horse that is 100 percent one breed or another. A Thoroughbred horse belongs to a particular breed–the fastest breed in the world.

Bred as Race Horses

Thoroughbreds are bred as race horses in the United States, England, and other countries. There are other animals, even other horses, that can run faster for short distances. But no animal on earth can run as fast for as long as a Thoroughbred.

"Only after you see a Thoroughbred run," says a horse expert, "can you say that you know what speed really is. These horses don't just run. There's a much better word for what Thoroughbreds do. They *fly* around a track!"

Where did this astounding horse come from? How are Thoroughbred horses different from other fast horses? And what makes the Thoroughbred horse a winner in competition today?

Chapter 2

The History of
the Thoroughbred

Unlike some breeds that have existed for
thousands of years, the Thoroughbred horse is
a fairly new breed. About 300 years ago, some
people in England tried to "create" a new kind
of horse. They would cross two kinds of
horses, each of which had certain strengths.
The foal, or baby horse, would combine the
best of both breeds.

Needing a New Kind of Horse

The English nobles of that time owned large and heavy horses. These animals descended from the big horses that **knights** used to ride into battle. Speed was not important to the fighting knights. If a horse was strong enough to carry a man in armor, it was a good horse.

But now there were no more knights fighting on horseback. Soldiers could use crossbows, and later guns, to easily defeat men in armor. Instead of fighting, the nobles of the 17th century liked to race and hunt instead. They wanted horses with great speed.

The fastest horses in those days were Arabians, and they were hard to find. Arabs depended on these horses in their desert fighting. They didn't want to lose them. In some parts of the Middle East, it was even a crime for an Arab to sell his horse.

And even though the Arabians were fast, they were small. The English wanted a fast horse, but also one with strength. By breeding

their English horses to Arabians, they could get an ideal combination of size and speed.

The Coming of the Arabians

Between 1680 and 1725, three Arabian stallions arrived in England. The first was a fast horse from Turkey. A Captain Byerly had used him as a war horse in Ireland. This horse–known today as the *Byerly Turk*–later retired to England.

The second was the *Darley Arabian*. An Englishman named Thomas Darley bought the horse in a secret deal in Syria. In 1704 Darley brought the reddish-brown horse to England, where the horse lived for 30 years.

The third horse, the *Godolphin Arabian*, was a gift from a nobleman in Morocco to the king of France. Somehow—no one knows exactly how—a wood **peddlar** bought the horse. The peddlar used him to pull a heavy cart through the streets of Paris. Later, he was sent to the farm of the Earl of Godolphin in England.

The Foundations of a New Breed

These three stallions—the *Byerly Turk*, the *Darley Arabian*, and the *Godolphin Arabian*—were bred to English mares. Their foals were quite different from the foals of either breed. They had the long legs and strength of the big English horses. They also had the blazing speed and **agility** of the Arabians. They were the first of a new breed—the Thoroughbred horse.

Chapter 3

The Development of the Thoroughbred

In the 18th century, horse breeders in England worked hard with the descendants of the country's first Arabians. They saw which Thoroughbred foals were the fastest and the strongest. The breeders chose these foals to mate with other outstanding Thoroughbreds. In this way, the breed improved.

A Famous Great-Great-Grandson

Almost all of the new Thoroughbred horses were fast. There was one horse, however, that really amazed the horse experts. His name was *Eclipse*. He was born in 1764 and was the great-great-grandson of the *Darley Arabian*.

Eclipse was not the most beautiful Thoroughbred in England. He seemed awkward and clumsy. And he did not get along with other horses. If another horse approached, *Eclipse* would flatten his ears and snap his teeth angrily. If someone tried to ride him, he would rear up and toss the rider off his back. When *Eclipse* began racing, however, he turned out to be the best horse around.

Eclipse never finished lower than first place in any race! In his 18 months of racing, he beat every horse he ran against, usually by a long distance. He was so much faster than other horses, in fact, that there was a saying in his day: "*Eclipse* first, the rest nowhere."

Eclipse produced more than racing trophies and medals. He **sired**, or fathered, 400 foals after he stopped racing. They became racing champions and the ancestors of the modern Thoroughbred. In fact, 98 percent of all

modern Thoroughbred horses can trace their roots back to *Eclipse*!

The Rise of Horse Racing

As Thoroughbred horses improved, the sport of horse racing grew. It became known as the "sport of kings," because so many kings and princes enjoyed it. The English king Charles II even raced his own race horse!

Races in England at that time were quite different from modern Thoroughbred races. Only two horses raced at a time. The winners of each **heat** ran against each other, until there was only one horse left–the winner. Since the length of a single heat was about 4 miles (5.4 kilometers), winning race horses ran between 12 and 20 miles (16.2 and 27 kilometers) before the racing day was over!

Winning Thoroughbred horses were fast. They had big chests and strong lungs, and they seemed to gain speed with each new race. These lightning-fast horses made horse racing more popular than ever before.

The Thoroughbred in America

The Thoroughbred did not remain completely English. Settlers from England brought racing horses to America with them. *Bulle Rock*, the first Thoroughbred in the colonies, arrived in 1730. He was a son of the *Darley Arabian*.

Americans were interested in breeding Thoroughbreds, too. Kentucky, with its mild climate and lush **bluegrass**, became an unofficial center of Thoroughbred horse breeding in America. It started in 1775, when the famous frontiersman Daniel Boone suggested that Kentuckians try horse breeding.

Americans enjoyed a different kind of horse race than the English. Americans liked speed. They enjoyed watching their horses go at top speed for a mile or two. The long English race was just not fast enough for them.

In the shorter American races, horses had to go at full speed from start to finish. There was no need for endurance, because all the horses ran together in a single heat. So American horse owners tried to breed Thoroughbreds that could put on a strong burst of speed.

Chapter 4

The Thoroughbred Today

All Thoroughbred horses in England are registered, as they have been since the breed became "official" in 1831. In the United States, the American Jockey Club registers Thoroughbreds. An officially registered horse has a number **tattooed** inside its upper lip. The number ensures that one horse can never race in place of another.

A registered horse also must have an official name that no other race horse has. This name is not always the horse's everyday name. But if the Thoroughbred ever enters a race, the horse's official name must be used.

"We call my horse Lucky," says one Thoroughbred owner. "But it wasn't a race-horse name. Her racing name is Luckless Monday. But to me she will always be Lucky!"

Physical Characteristics of a Thoroughbred

Thoroughbreds are much taller than most horses. All horses are measured in four-inch (10-centimeter) segments called hands, from the **withers** (the top of a horse's shoulders) to the ground. A full-grown Thoroughbred stands between 15 and 17 hands.

Even though they are tall, Thoroughbreds are not big-boned or heavy. In fact, the horse is rather light–between 900 and 1200 pounds (408 and 544 kilograms). There is power in the Thoroughbred horse's body, but no bulk.

Thoroughbreds are known for their good looks as well as their speed. They have large eyes and alert ears. Big nostrils help the animal gulp in as much air as possible.

(Horses can only breathe through their noses. They don't breathe through their mouths like humans.)

The Thoroughbred horse comes in many colors, including brown, gray, and roan (solid color with white hairs mixed in). Many Thoroughbreds are **bays** (reddish brown with black legs, main, and tail) and chestnuts (reddish brown with no black markings). A pure white or pure black Thoroughbred is rare.

The Age of a Thoroughbred

Horses' ages are usually figured the same way as human ages: from birthday to birthday. This is not so with Thoroughbred horses. The 50,000 Thoroughbreds born each year in the United States all have the same

birthday–January 1. The American Jockey
Club gives all foals born in the same year the
same birthday. This is so the horses can be
more easily organized for races in which only
one age group competes.

Chapter 5

The Thoroughbred in Action

Some horses are for work. Some are for pleasure riding. Racing is what Thoroughbreds do best. There are many opportunities for Thoroughbreds to race in the United States and Canada.

The Kentucky Derby

The most famous race in the world is called the Kentucky Derby. It is held each year at Churchill Downs, Kentucky, on the first Saturday in May. Like many other races, the

Kentucky Derby is for three-year-olds.
(Thoroughbreds do not begin racing until they
are two years old. Their growing muscles and
bones could be injured if they ran at full speed
any earlier.)

The Kentucky Derby is the first of three
important races called the Triple Crown. The
second race, called the Preakness, is run at

Pimlico, a track in Baltimore, Maryland. The third is the Belmont Stakes, run at Belmont Park in New York.

The Triple Crown

The Triple Crown races take place in a six-week period. This can be difficult for trainers and horses. The races have been run for more

than a century. In that time only 11 horses have won all three races in the Triple Crown.

The Purse

The winners of each race collect a **purse**, or prize money. The winners of the Triple Crown gain a special honor. Their names will go down in racing history because they have accomplished something few others have.

Dangers for Race Horses

There are risks for the Thoroughbred horses that compete in races. Some horses bleed from their noses during a race, because their hard breathing breaks the blood vessels in their nose. The horse can choke on the blood.

Instead of waiting for the injury to heal, some owners give their horses medicine to stop the bleeding. This medicine does not really cure the problem. The vessels may still be broken or weak. The horse may injure them even more severely the next time it races.

Pain Killers

Pain-killing drugs are another problem in the racing industry. A horse with a hurt leg or another injury can be hurt worse if such drugs are given. The medicine lets the horse put weight on the injured leg without feeling pain. This can make the injury even worse.

Experts say that horse owners have paid too little attention to such issues. Some claim that because horse racing brings in so much money,

owners and racing officials don't want to change things. Greedy owners may be willing to risk a horse's health to get a few more races out of it.

Help from the AHPA

Many people are trying to solve these problems. The American Horse Protection Association, or AHPA, is one group of

concerned horse lovers. The AHPA is working hard to keep horses healthy and safe. They educate new owners of Thoroughbreds about proper care. They also try to persuade government officials to pass strong laws protecting horses.

More than Racing

Even though Thoroughbreds have been bred for racing, there are other ways people enjoy them. Some Thoroughbreds take part in a special kind of riding called dressage. In dressage the horse learns to follow the complicated commands of its rider. The commands tell the horse to move at a walk or a **canter**, and even which foot to start on! In dressage competitions, officials judge horses and riders in action.

Other Things Thoroughbreds Do

Thoroughbred horses are also used in polo matches and in jumping contests. "There are lots of things Thoroughbreds can do besides race," says one owner. "They love to run.

And they are agile. I compete with my horse, but I also love to just saddle him up and take him for a morning ride."

People–and even some Thoroughbred owners–are surprised when they learn the many things the horses can do well. It seems that the more people learn about Thoroughbreds, the more they appreciate this special horse.

Glossary

agility–the ability to move quickly and easily

bay–a reddish-brown horse, with black legs, mane, and tail

bluegrass–a healthy grass grown in Kentucky for horse pastures

bran–a food for horses made from grain

canter–a slow running pace

chestnut–a reddish brown horse, with no dark markings

dressage–a competition in which horses receive complicated commands from their riders. Judges evaluate how well horse and rider communicate.

foal–a young horse

hand–a unit of measurement equal to four inches (10 centimeters)

heat–a single race in a competition made up of several races

knights–soldiers on horseback

mare–a female horse

peddlar–one who sells inexpensive items to the public by traveling from place to place

pinto–a multicolored horse, often white and brown

polo–a sport played by two teams of riders and their horses

purebred–a horse that is 100 percent one breed

purse–the money prize in a horse race

roan–a solid color coat with white hairs mixed in

sire–the father of a horse

stallion–a male horse

tattoo–a permanent mark or number made on the skin

withers–the top of a horse's shoulders

To Learn More

Callahan, Dorothy. *Thoroughbreds.* Mankato, MN: Crestwood House, 1983.

Clutton-Brock, Juliet. *Horse.* New York: Alfred A. Knopf, 1992.

Johnson, Neil. *Born to Run: A Racehorse Grows Up.* New York: Scholastic, 1988.

McFarland, Cynthia. *Hoofbeats: The Story of a Thoroughbred.* New York: Atheneum, 1993.

Patent, Dorothy Hinshaw. *Horses of America.* New York: Holiday House, 1981.

You can read articles about Thoroughbred horses in these magazines: *Thoroughbred Times*, *Horse Illustrated*, and *Horse and Rider*.

Some Useful Addresses

Canadian Thoroughbred Horse Society
Société canadienne du cheval thoroughbred
P.O. Box 172
Rexdale, ON M9W 5L1

American Horse Protection Association
1000-29th Street NW
Washington, DC 20007

Thoroughbred Racing Association
300 Marcus Avenue, Suite 2W4
Lake Success, NY 11042

The Kentucky Derby Museum
700 Central Avenue
Louisville, KY 40201

The National Museum of Racing and National Horse Racing Museum
Union Avenue
Saratoga Springs, NY 12866

Index

American Horse Protection Association, 38, 41
American Jockey Club, 4, 25, 29
Arabian horses, 4, 12-14, 17
Arabs, 12
armor, 12

Baltimore, Maryland, 33
Belmont Park, 33
Belmont Stakes, 33
bluegrass, 22
Boone, Daniel, 22
breathing, 26-27, 36
breeding, 4, 5, 8, 11-14, 17, 22
Bulle Rock, 22

Byerly, Captain, 13
Byerly Turk, the, 13-14

Canada, 31
Charles II, 21
colors, 4, 27
competitions, 5, 41

Darley, Thomas, 14
Darley Arabian, the, 14, 18, 22
diet, 5
dressage, 41
drugs, 36

Eclipse, 18, 20-21
England, 4, 8, 11-14, 21-22, 25
English horses, 4, 12-14